W9-BON-062

CONTENTS

THE

THREE
HABITS
OF HIGHLY
CONTAGIOUS
CHRISTIANS

Other Resources by Garry Poole

The Complete Book of Questions
Seeker Small Groups

In the Tough Questions Series:

Don't All Religions Lead to God?
How Could God Allow Suffering and Evil?
How Does Anyone Know God Exists?
Why Become a Christian?
Tough Questions Leader's Guide (with Judson Poling)

THE

THREE
HABITS
OF HIGHLY
CONTAGIOUS
CHRISTIANS

A Discussion Guide for Small Groups

GARRY POOLE

foreword by **Bill Hybels**

GRAND RAPIDS, MICHIGAN 49530 USA

We want to hear from you. Please send your comments about this book to us in care of zreview@zondervan.com. Thank you.

ZONDERVAN™

The Three Habits of Highly Contagious Christians
Copyright © 2003 by Willow Creek Association

Requests for information should be addressed to:

Zondervan, *Grand Rapids, Michigan 49530*

ISBN-10: 0-310-24496-X (softcover)
ISBN-13: 978-0-310-24496-7 (softcover)

All Scripture quotations, unless otherwise indicated, are taken from the *New American Standard Bible,* © 1960, 1962, 1963, 1968, 1971, 1972, 1973, 1975, 1977 by the Lockman Foundation. Used by permission.

Scripture quotations marked NIV are taken from the *Holy Bible New International Version®.* NIV®. Copyright © 1973, 1978, 1984 by the International Bible Society. Used by permission of Zondervan. All rights reserved.

Interior design by Tracey Moran

Printed in the United States of America

05 06 07 08 09 10 /❖ CH/ 12 11 10 9 8 7 6 5 4

FOREWORD

Lost people matter. This phrase reflects the heart of God and the heartbeat of Willow Creek Community Church. It's why we work so hard to build relationships with people who are far from God, put together high-impact services, and communicate the Gospel creatively and clearly. We have been seized by the vision that God wants to use our lives, our relationships, our words, and our collective efforts to impact the people around us for all of eternity.

And as fully devoted followers of Christ, we are called upon to fulfill our redemptive potential. It's our job, according to Luke 15, to search high and low as we go wherever we need to go and do whatever we need to do to reach people throughout our spheres of influence. People with names and faces. People we care about deeply. People in our families, our neighborhoods, our workplaces, and our schools. And it takes each of us doing our part, with God's help, to reach those all around us.

Can you be counted on? Are you in? Will you enroll in this great redemptive adventure? I believe it's what you want to do. There's no greater endeavor. There's nothing your seeking friends need more. There's nothing that would better please the heart of God.

How do you start? That's the question this book will help you answer. Willow Creek's long-time evangelism director, Garry Poole, has distilled his years of experience and expertise into this simple, yet powerful discussion guide. So now, within the context and safety of your small group, you can encourage each other and cheer each other on to put into practice the three habits of highly contagious Christians.

So push the pause button on whatever it is your group is doing now and follow this outstanding guide—study it, discuss it, digest it, and apply it to your everyday life. Focus well, pray hard, and even take some risks. God will reach many people who matter to him—and he will do it through you.

Bill Hybels
Senior Pastor
Willow Creek Community Church

INTRODUCTION

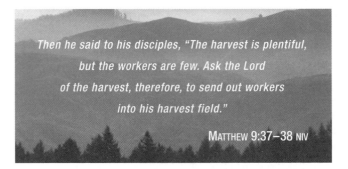

Then he said to his disciples, "The harvest is plentiful,
but the workers are few. Ask the Lord
of the harvest, therefore, to send out workers
into his harvest field."

MATTHEW 9:37–38 NIV

Without question, Jesus Christ calls every one of his followers to live an intentionally contagious Christian life. His great concern and compassion is to reach out to "the sheep without a shepherd." In John 10:14–16, his words are filled with emotion for lost people: "I am the good shepherd; and I know My own, and My own know Me . . . and I lay down My life for the sheep. And I have other sheep, which are not of this fold; I must bring them also, and they shall hear My voice; and they shall become one flock with one shepherd." Can you empathize with his deep passion for this broken world, to make us all one under his loving watchful care? Most of us can identify with his great commission, yet we struggle with where to start or how to stay motivated. Living out his call to share the life-giving Good News is a big challenge, and sometimes all we lack are some practical steps and tools to help us get going.

Welcome to *The Three Habits of Highly Contagious Christians.* You and your small group are about to embark on an exciting journey filled with possibility. The three sessions included in this guide have been specifically designed to sharpen your thinking about reaching out to seekers for Christ—and to ignite your heart to do it. Throughout each session, you will discuss practical ways to make a difference in the lives of people you know. Few things in life are as important as implementing the habits to become highly contagious.

Those of us here at Willow Creek Community Church are so serious about turning irreligious people into fully devoted followers of Jesus Christ that we've developed a seven-step strategy that you also can use as a guide in your evangelistic efforts. Here are the seven steps:

1. **Build a Relationship**
2. **Share a Verbal Witness**
3. **Invite Seekers to Outreach Events, Seeker Small Groups, and Church Services**
4. Attend Worship and Bible Teaching Services
5. Participate in a Small Group
6. Serve in the Body of Christ
7. Steward Financial Resources

This discussion guide for small groups is based on the first three steps of this strategy; those steps are a practical approach for getting intentional in our efforts to effectively reach people who will otherwise face a Christ-less eternity. Over the years, these steps have been proven to be a powerful and effective way to reach out and help many people who do not know Christ cross the line of faith.

Each session takes a thorough look at how to become active in taking one of these three steps. These steps are not always easy, and they are not without their struggles and setbacks. But if we persevere together and trust God to use us however he chooses, the gains for the Kingdom will be well worth the price.

This introductory guide will most likely whet your appetite for more in-depth training, so everyone participating in this study should also consider taking an evangelism training course as a supplement to what is provided here. The *Becoming a Contagious Christian* course and the *Seeker Small Groups* book are resources designed for this very purpose.

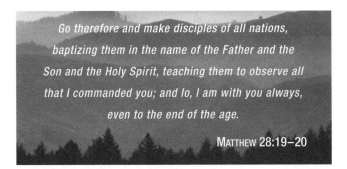

Go therefore and make disciples of all nations, baptizing them in the name of the Father and the Son and the Holy Spirit, teaching them to observe all that I commanded you; and lo, I am with you always, even to the end of the age.

MATTHEW 28:19–20

Using This Guide

The three sessions in this discussion guide consist primarily of questions to be answered in a group setting. The questions are designed to provoke honest, open discussion rather than short, simple answers. Each participant should have his or her own guide to follow along in the discussion, and each person should come to the group meeting having already read through the session to be discussed. Space is provided for jotting down thoughts and ideas to share with the other participants. Groups should designate a leader or facilitator who can keep discussions focused and well paced.

Defining the Terms

In order to maintain clarity and consistency throughout each group discussion, certain terms need to be understood and remembered. First, a person is considered to be a non-Christian—no matter where that person is in his or her spiritual journey—if he or she has not crossed the line of faith and accepted Christ. In addition, the terms *seeker, seeking friend, non-Christian, unchurched,* and *irreligious* are used interchangeably and are, for the purposes of this study, one and the same. These terms signify any person who has not yet personally received Jesus Christ as forgiver and leader—regardless of whether or not the person is actually in the process of seeking God.

Outreach events are defined as special functions specifically geared to help non-Christians take steps along their spiritual journeys. These events, hosted at churches or other venues, include a wide variety of formats—from Christian music concerts to question-and-answer forums with Christian apologetics experts. Seeker small groups are defined as communities of two to twelve seekers plus one or two Christian leaders who gather in homes, workplaces, or churches on a regular basis, primarily to discuss spiritual matters. My book *Seeker Small Groups* provides detailed coaching about how to effectively launch these specialized outreach groups.

The Introduction

Each session begins with a short story. Although the names and some of the details have been altered for simplicity and clarity, these stories are based on actual events and experiences. Some group members may have read these beforehand, but the group should take a few minutes to read the story together at the beginning of each meeting. Vary how this is done from meeting to meeting. One week someone in the group might read it out loud; another time, members could each read a section. These readings are intended to set the stage for the group discussion and should spark ideas for putting into practice each of the three habits of highly contagious Christians.

Open for Discussion

Once the introduction has been read, it's time to get into the core of the session: the discussion questions. Each session contains ten to twelve questions. You may not get through all of the questions, so the leader may want to predetermine which ones to spend more time on, based on the needs of the individuals in the group. Some groups may decide to spend more than one meeting on each session. In any case, the important thing is to engage everyone in the discussion, using the questions to draw one another out and give everyone the opportunity to wrestle with the challenges and discoveries. Encourage group members to honestly identify, in a nonjudgmental atmosphere, the deeper issues behind their own barriers to reaching out to lost people.

Heart Check

This section represents a slight turn in the group discussion. Generally speaking, the questions in this part of the session speak more to the emotional or motivational facet of the issue, rather than the intellectual "how to" part. As a group, try to encourage one another to discover satisfying and motivating answers for both the mind and heart.

Personal Profile

A true story from my own personal experience is threaded throughout all three sessions. It is included as a means to further illustrate the principles and habits outlined in this guide.

Charting Your Journey

The purpose of this section is to help everyone in the group go one step beyond discussion toward personal application. This group experience is, after all, a journey—so each session includes at least one section devoted to helping people talk about their next steps. *This may well be the most important part of each group meeting.* Here is an opportunity, before God and each other, to individually commit to a specific action step that could make all the difference in the lives of seeking friends and family members. Don't miss this defining moment with your group.

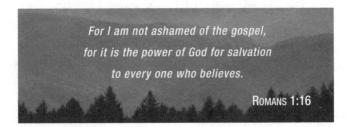

> For I am not ashamed of the gospel,
> for it is the power of God for salvation
> to every one who believes.
>
> ROMANS 1:16

Final Matters

Living an intentionally contagious Christian life really matters. It matters to our heavenly Father who gave up the life of his Son to buy back the ones he loves so much. It desperately matters to all those who are yet to be redeemed from a Christ-less eternity. It matters to our churches as we strive to fulfill our redemptive potential. It is, without doubt, worth all the effort and risks involved. So let's devote ourselves to the three habits of highly contagious Christians. Only eternity will tell just how much it matters.

May your efforts and your faithfulness honor God—and in so doing, you will be forever grateful.

HANG OUT TOGETHER

Building Relationships with Seekers

Jeff and I are next-door neighbors. When he and his family moved in about a year ago, my wife and I went over to welcome them to the neighborhood.

At first, that was the extent of our interaction since my time was limited and I really didn't want to add any more people to my already full life. I was very involved with the guys in my small group Bible study, I played in a church basketball league every Monday night with my four closest friends, and my wife and I socialized on a regular basis with the Christian couple across the street. Besides, it was obvious from the start that Jeff and I had different sets of values and morals. So I was reluctant to complicate my life with someone who was the polar opposite of everything I was or wanted to be and assumed our differences would make things awkward.

Unbelievably, that has all changed. One day, I decided to start praying for Jeff on a regular basis, and to my surprise, I found myself viewing him as someone who really matters to God—and to *me*. I began looking for ways to reach out and to get to know him better, and eventually got to the point where I started to genuinely care about the guy.

To top it off, I discovered that we had lots of things in common after all. We both follow sports pretty closely, so it was natural for us to get tickets to the Bears games at Soldier Field. When one of us needed help with a project around the house, the other was right there to pitch in. Now, whether it's a neighborhood block party, the Fourth of July, or just a picnic in the backyard, somehow we wind up together. We sincerely enjoy hanging out with each other, and I feel we have a pretty solid friendship. I can't get over how helpful Jeff has been to my family and me. When we're away on vacation or a business trip, he mows the lawn, grabs the mail, and checks on the house for us. And I can't count how many times this past winter I've come home late to find Jeff shoveling my driveway.

Early on in our friendship, Jeff confided in me that he was struggling in his job and was looking to make a change. Without hesitation, I gave Jeff a small clue about my relationship with God by letting him know I'd pray for him and his situation. When he ended up landing the job he'd been hoping for, he made a joke about my "special connection upstairs." That's when I gently inquired about any "connections" *he* had with God and confirmed that, although Jeff and his wife attend church from time to time, they probably were not Christians. We would, however, talk about spiritual issues occasionally, and I looked forward to those opportunities.

One such discussion went on late into the night after dinner at his house. Jeff's wife, Amy, concluded our dialogue with an amazing challenge. She said she'd recently wanted to get a Bible study started in our neighborhood, but hadn't felt that she or anyone she knew could lead it.

She wondered out loud if my wife and I would consider doing such a thing. "Maybe," I calmly replied as my heart pounded. I couldn't believe my own ears!

Yesterday, I was cutting the grass in my backyard when Jeff suddenly appeared out of nowhere and signaled me to cut the engine. He had just gotten off the phone with a cousin who had been hounding him to no end about Christianity. After declining an invitation to attend church for the umpteenth time, Jeff had received some "inside information" about me, his friendly neighbor! I wondered where in the world he was going with this. "My cousin told me you go to the same church he does," Jeff explained, "and since we're neighbors, he's hoping that maybe *you'll* be the one to finally convert me." *Thud.* I felt like crawling into a hole.

Jeff just stood there with eyebrows raised, waiting for my reaction. I frantically tried to smooth things over by explaining that I wasn't really trying to "convert" Jeff, but was simply open to talking with him about something that has come to mean so much to me. He turned to walk away, and I feared the worst. But then Jeff stopped and slowly turned with a smile.

"So, man ... am I your church project or your friend?"

> But we proved to be gentle among you, as a nursing mother tenderly cares for her own children. Having thus a fond affection for you, we were well-pleased to impart to you not only the gospel of God but also our own lives, because you had become very dear to us.
>
> 1 THESSALONIANS 2:7–8

Open for Discussion

1. Share the first name of a spiritual seeker (non-believer) you know fairly well. What is your relationship like? If you are unable to identify someone in your world who's seeking, what's something you could do to change that?

2. What motivates you to initiate and build friendships with seekers?

   What are the greatest obstacles that hinder the development of these friendships?

3. What fears and concerns do you suppose seekers might have about being friends with Christians? (Come up with as many of these fears and concerns as you can.)

4. Keeping the fears and concerns you just identified in mind, what might a seeker need from you to ensure that the relationship is going to be a safe one?

    How would you rate your ability to create a safe context for such a relationship?

5. Read 1 Corinthians 9:19, 22–23. A basic ingredient to building meaningful relationships with seekers is a growing level of trust within those friendships. What can you do to build bridges of trust within the context of growing friendships with your seeking friends?

    What could dismantle the bridges of trust between you and seekers?

Use the chart below to list the responses you and your group members come up with.

TRUST BUILDERS	TRUST BUSTERS

6. One of the most effective ways you can develop growing, authentic friendships with seekers is to identify areas of common interest, and then spend time together doing those things. For you and your seeking friends, what activities would those be? What specific steps will you take to initiate time together?

Heart Check

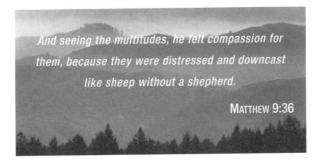

And seeing the multitudes, he felt compassion for them, because they were distressed and downcast like sheep without a shepherd.

MATTHEW 9:36

7. Read the Scripture in the box above. What did Jesus see when he looked at seekers?

How does Jesus' compassion impact you?

Is your response filled with feelings of motivation or guilt? Explain.

In what ways does your heart need to change in order for you to begin to see seekers through the eyes of Jesus?

8. Read 1 Thessalonians 2:7–8 in the box on page 17. It has been said that seekers don't care how much you know until they know how much you care. What are some ways you can authentically demonstrate your care for someone who is spiritually seeking?

9. Identify the two or three seekers you hope to see cross the line of faith someday. Use the Impact List on page 55 to remind you to pray for them on a regular basis.

Take some time now as a group to pray about your heart and attitude toward those seekers in your life, as well as your personal efforts to spend time with them.

Personal Profile

I first met Jay in middle school. As we began to hang out together, we would occasionally look each other straight in the eye and see both a friend and a competitor. We were in a lot of the same classes, where we would battle for the better grades. As it turned out, we both played trumpet in the band, and time after time we would shoot each other a grin before vying for the higher chair by playing a piece for the band director. "Jay, you're outta here," I'd say as I headed for the music room. And I'd beat him—only to be outdone by him the next time!

Most of all, we enjoyed competing in sports—baseball, wrestling, football—to list just a few. We thoroughly enjoyed this friendly kind of warfare; he'd slap me on the back as we entered the gym for a wrestling match and say, "Hey man, you're such a good friend, I'll almost feel bad when I pin you in ten seconds flat!" During our baseball games, if I picked up a bat and hit a home run, you'd better believe Jay would try his best to do the same. And if he snagged a fly ball with an impressive dive, I'd run all the harder to make an even more aggressive catch. Whatever the activity, we turned up the competitive heat.

But there was only one thing we didn't have in common—faith. I was a Christian; Jay, an atheist. By the time we were in high school, Jay was quite vocal about this major difference between us. And he didn't have any hesitation mentioning this fact to all who would listen. "God is just a figment of your imagination for your own convenience, to pacify you," he'd state. "There is no God. It's just something your parents talked about to scare you—and foolishly, you bought into it." It was almost like he was some kind of "atheistic evangelist."

Even in this area, our competitive natures emerged. As Jay eagerly explained his lack of belief in God, I openly told each others about the God I trusted and followed. We were equally confident about our own stance and demonstrated a strong conviction for what we believed. Yet, it was hard for me to fathom how someone with whom I had so much in common could feel so differently—exactly the opposite direction—about God.

One day, a group of us were on a road trip to a sporting event, and Jay decided to make things interesting. He had already gained a reputation for being an animated guy who enjoyed stirring up a crowd, so it didn't surprise any of us when he began to liven up our long bus ride through the flat farmland of northern Indiana.

He stood up in the front of the bus and yelled out a challenge. "Listen you guys. To make this ride more interesting, I think we should split up and have a big debate. So, whoever believes in God, sit on this side, and whoever doesn't believe God exists, sit on the other side." Curiosity—and an appreciation for Jay's courage and creativity—split us up just as he suggested. As we shifted from one side to the other, Jay continued. "I'll represent all the atheists, and Garry here will represent those of you who believe in God. Let's settle this once and for all!"

I went along with the idea and stood up next to Jay. Surprisingly, there were an equal number of kids on both sides of the aisle, and for the rest of the trip, that entire busload of students engaged in an exciting, intense discussion about the existence of God. I no longer remember all the specific arguments, but I do know that convictions ran deep and emotions were charged.

10. Read the personal profile above and identify the areas of common ground between Jay and the author as well as any hints that indicate that they really enjoyed their friendship.

11. Describe a seeker in your life with whom you have something in common and have the potential to spend time together. Dream out loud about what that scenario might look like to you. What's preventing you from taking steps to fulfill that dream?

Charting Your Journey

With this session, you're beginning a journey. And it could be the start of something thrilling as you learn to cultivate bridges of trust with your seeking friends. Just think about what God could do through you to reach the lost for him. So take full advantage of these sessions: ask the hard questions, think "outside the box," and learn from what others in your group have to say. Just be authentic about where you are in the process.

To help you apply what you're learning, the Charting Your Journey sections are designed to provide opportunities for you to indicate specific next steps in your process of reaching out to the seekers in your life. Don't be overly concerned if you are not yet where you want to be—it's a process. And this exercise is a step in the right direction. Progress takes time, but the important thing is for you to be open about where you are now and where you want to be in the near future.

12. Check any of the statements below that describe the specific next steps you would like to work on and apply in your life at this point. Share your selection with the rest of the group and give reasons for your response.

❑ I will prayerfully identify by name the seekers I hope to see cross the line of faith, and I will pray for them every day.

❑ Hanging out with seekers will become a higher priority in my life. I will arrange to spend time with a seeking friend this week.

❑ I will get more intentional about initiating activities with my seeking friends. I will block out some time to be with seekers each week over the next month.

❑ I really don't have any seeking friends in my life, and I'd like to change that. I will prayerfully initiate contact with a seeker and strive to form an authentic friendship with that person.

❑ My heart needs to be softened toward seekers. This month I will pray and study God's Word about developing a heart for the lost.

❑ I will identify and ask God to help me change the things I do that tend to drive seekers away from me.

❑ I will identify a need in the life of a seeking friend and reach out to meet that need this week.

❑ I will identify an area of common interest and regularly pursue that interest with my seeking friend.

❑ I want to see seekers through the eyes of Jesus. This week, as I see and interact with seekers in my world, I will pray for them and ask God to help me to see them as he does.

❑ Write your own phrase that describes a specific next step you will take in building relationships with seekers here:

Now go back through the above exercise and select the one action item you intend to implement first. Write that sentence in the space provided on page 57 of this guide.

LOOK FOR OPEN WINDOWS

Sharing a Verbal Witness with Seekers

Last year my husband, Mike, and I were in the market for a new car. Now, I have a thing for cars, so I was particularly excited about test driving lots of different models. But the ones I liked most, believe it or not, were those shiny new Ford Mustangs. So during our month of car shopping, I took advantage of every opportunity to take one out for a spin.

Throughout that month, I noticed something kind of funny. Whenever Mike and I were out driving around town, we would spot all kinds of other Ford Mustangs on the road! It seemed like we'd see them everywhere we looked. We'd notice the color, the condition it was in, the specific model—even what it was loaded with, when we could tell. It actually became this running joke between us: Mike would yell, "There's your car, Hon," or "Hey, who's that driving your car?" I'd look over and sure enough, there'd be another variety of my favorite Ford. Soon it got to the point where the only cars we seemed to notice were Ford Mustangs.

Well, as it turned out, we ended up purchasing a Pontiac Grand Prix, and the strangest thing started to happen.

Wouldn't you know it—Mike and I now spot my Pontiac Grand Prix everywhere. And we never notice any Ford Mustangs. Are they even on the road anymore?

Come to find out, there's a logical explanation behind our humorous little mind game. The other day I discovered that there's this portion of the brain called the reticular activating center. It's a mouthful, I know, but evidently this little section is what's responsible for triggering our minds like that. It somehow alerts us to whatever stimuli that we (either consciously or subconsciously) have previously programmed it to notice. So, our reticular activating centers were simply flipping those switches to pick up on and respond to whichever car we were most interested in at the time.

Well, for me there's something really significant about this discovery. Recently, I've been fascinated by the fact that I can put my reticular activating center to work for me. I have found that I can sort of "preprogram" my mind to be on the lookout for windows of opportunity to engage my seeking friends in conversations about spiritual things. I have never realized before how many times a day I let those opportunities slip by simply because I was not looking for them. I had lost my awareness of opportunities to gently turn the conversation toward spiritual things and to go just a little bit deeper with a seeker about his or her spiritual journey. Through prayer, God has helped me adjust my focus and shift my priorities. I've determined to activate my mind to flag those opportunities and bring them to the forefront of my thinking.

Sometimes the windows are open only a short time. But now I actually see them, when before I didn't even notice. And so, as I sense God's Spirit leading, I've been prayerfully and very carefully asking my seeker friends more probing spiritual questions or gently dropping more clues about my interest in spiritual matters. If the window gets abruptly shut, that's okay. I just respectfully back off. But there have been a few times when, much to my surprise, the window of opportunity flings wide open, and I find myself deeply engaged with a seeker about eternal concerns. It's now my passion in life to always be ready to take advantage of the open windows of opportunity God brings my way. And it's become the thrill of a lifetime.

> *Devote yourselves to prayer, keeping alert in it with an attitude of thanksgiving; praying at the same time for us as well, that God may open up to us a door for the word, so that we may speak forth the mystery of Christ . . . in order that I may make it clear in the way I ought to speak.*
>
> COLOSSIANS 4:2–4

Open for Discussion

1. Does your reticular activating center flag opportunities to turn conversations with your seeker friends toward spiritual things? Using the scale below, select a number from one to ten that best describes your awareness level of such opportunities. What reasons do you have for choosing that number?

1	**2**	**3**	**4**	**5**	**6**	**7**	**8**	**9**	**10**

I never even notice any opportunities.	Sometimes I'm aware of opportunities.	I am alerted to every opportunity that arises.

2. What are some things you could do to improve your awareness level of the open windows of opportunity that come your way?

Drop Clues Right Away

Two acquaintances worked at the same office complex for an entire year before they discovered they were both Christians. Why? Neither one had ever offered any clues about their spiritual interests and involvement. They had never even mentioned that they attended church or had kids in the church youth program or were involved in a Bible study. These kinds of hints about our spiritual lives are simple ways to identify ourselves with Christ, and the longer we put off sharing these spiritual clues, the harder it becomes to do so later. As hanging out with seekers builds bridges of trust, dropping clues about your interest in spiritual matters builds platforms from which you can eventually launch deeper discussions about the Christian message.

3. What are some examples of spiritual clues you can use with the seekers you know?

What hinders you from casually commenting about your spiritual life and interests with seekers?

Why does it become harder to drop clues the longer you wait?

Seize the Opportunity

It's one thing to be aware of our windows of opportunity, but it's quite another to seize them. So here's the deal: As you consistently *hang out together* with seekers and *drop clues right away* about your own spiritual life and interests, it's often just a matter of time until the window of opportunity opens right in front of you. And if you're willing to take the risk and seize the opportunity, you'll find yourself praying for wisdom as you carefully engage your seeker friends in heartfelt conversations about spiritual matters. Nothing can compare with the thrill of this awesome responsibility and privilege.

4. How prepared are you to initiate and carry on spiritual discussions once you've recognized an open window? Explain your answer.

What obstacles prevent you from feeling more confident about starting spiritual conversations? Share examples from your past experiences.

Heart Check

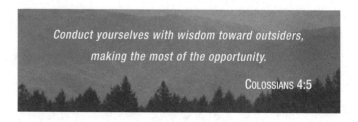

Conduct yourselves with wisdom toward outsiders, making the most of the opportunity.

COLOSSIANS 4:5

5. Read Colossians 4:5 above. There may be times when the only way a conversation about spiritual things will happen is if *you* get things started. Give some examples of probing questions or statements you could use to test the openness of seekers toward discussing spiritual topics at a deeper level.

As you think about actually initiating a spiritual conversation with seekers, what fears or hopes come to mind?

Does this pattern of sharing your faith seem to be a realistic possibility for your life? Why or why not?

Let your speech always be with grace, seasoned, as it were with salt, so that you may know how you should respond to each person.

COLOSSIANS 4:6

6. Read Colossians 4:6 on the previous page. As you're on the lookout, ready to make the most of any open windows, it's important not to force things to happen. Realize that you can only go as far into a spiritual discussion as seekers will allow; if the window of opportunity is only open a crack, seekers may sometimes respond by opening the window wider. Other times they may shut the window altogether. What signals tip you off that it's time to ease off the discussion?

Why is it important that you back off when a seeker closes the window?

Get the Message Down

Over the course of time, as you develop friendships with seekers and share spiritual conversations with them, you will eventually have a chance to explain the Gospel message. It is imperative that as a highly contagious Christian, you know the Gospel so well that you can share it in a clear and compelling way. So, get your preparation done. That can't be emphasized too much.

7. Using the scale below, select a number from one to ten that best describes how confident you are in your ability to clearly articulate the Gospel and assist a seeker to positively respond to Jesus Christ. What reasons do you have for choosing that number?

1	**2**	**3**	**4**	**5**	**6**	**7**	**8**	**9**	**10**

I am totally unprepared to explain the Gospel message.

I might be able to explain parts of the Gospel message.

I am totally prepared to clearly articulate the Gospel message.

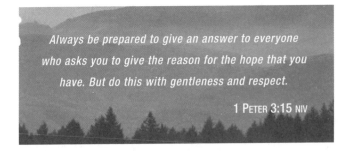

Always be prepared to give an answer to everyone who asks you to give the reason for the hope that you have. But do this with gentleness and respect.

1 PETER 3:15 NIV

8. Read 1 Peter 3:15 above. What steps could you take to better prepare yourself to clearly articulate the Gospel message? (Your small group might consider attending the next offering of an evangelism training course together.)

9. Study the Do vs. Done illustration of the Gospel message in the chart on page 56. Take a few minutes now to pair up and practice sharing this illustration with each other.

Personal Profile

The last week of our senior year, Jay and I, along with twenty other classmates, scrambled for our desks in our advanced math class and anxiously prepared to take the final exam. The teacher had not yet arrived, and Jay determined that if any of us were going to make it through this big test, what we really needed was some divine intervention. So he stood up in front of the class and led us in a kind of mock prayer. "Oh God, up there in the sky, I know you're not really there, but if you are, we sure could use your help with this final exam. Help us, help us, help us!" he implored. The whole class roared with laughter. We all knew Jay was an atheist and saw the irony of his plea. As Jay took his seat next to mine, I leaned over and whispered, "That was a mighty fine prayer for someone who doesn't even believe God exists."

Jay turned, looked me right in the eye, and said, "That was the first time in my life I ever said a prayer."

That summer Jay and I played a lot of tennis in the evenings at the local park. We had some pretty fierce games—including some very competitive doubles matches. But, typical of us, we were almost always on opposite teams. Often, our matches lasted late into the night.

By the time we finished, we'd frequently be the only two left on the courts. So we would shut off the lights, walk over to the parking lot, sit on the hoods of our cars, and just talk. We conversed about whatever was on our minds—you name it, we covered it.

Eventually, Jay would bring the conversation around to spiritual things. "Now you know I don't believe in God," he'd begin, "but if he *did* exist, why do you think. . . ." Then he would dive into some intellectual, spiritual issue. He seemed genuinely interested in exploring the implications of God's existence. I'd try my best to answer some of his disputes surrounding the existence of God, but I knew that his disbeliefs were deeply ingrained in his thinking. It would take, well, a *miracle* to change his mind.

At the time, I figured Jay's questions were random thoughts he had about Christianity. But looking back, I realize that his objections dealt mainly with the whole issue of God's existence and his miracles. In fact, Jay's concerns centered around the outlandish claims that make Christianity unique: God coming to the earth and living as a human being, even a baby; the resurrection of Jesus from the dead; and the entire concept of God's forgiveness secured by the death and resurrection of Christ. It was all too much—too supernatural and miraculous—for Jay to believe.

10. What windows of opportunity did the writer leverage to discuss spiritual matters with Jay?

11. In the past, what opportunities to discuss spiritual things have you either leveraged or let slip by?

How did you feel about those lost opportunities?

How can you ensure you make the most of every opportunity in the future?

12. Do you have an update about the seekers with whom you have been spending time and getting to know? Share any highlights. As a group, pray for open windows of opportunity to share the Gospel message with your seeker friends.

Charting Your Journey

13. Check any of the statements on the next page that describe the specific next steps you would like to work on and apply in your life at this point. Share your selection with the rest of the group and give reasons for your response.

- ❏ All week long, I will pray and look for opportunities to bring up spiritual matters with my seeker friends.
- ❏ I will deliberately take some risks in recognizing and taking advantage of open windows of opportunity and report back to the group what happened.
- ❏ I will do some reading over the next few weeks in order to prepare myself to answer difficult questions from seekers.
- ❏ I will do whatever it takes to learn how to explain the Gospel in a compelling way.
- ❏ I've talked with my seeking friends about spiritual matters before, but I will bring the topic up again this week.
- ❏ I will enroll in the next offering of an evangelism training course to improve my knowledge of how to explain both my story and God's story.
- ❏ As I hang out with seekers this week, I will intentionally drop clues about my faith and report back to the group what happened.
- ❏ I will identify and deal with my fears about sharing my faith with seekers.
- ❏ I will identify several questions I can ask seekers in order to draw them out about spiritual things.
- ❏ Write your own phrase that describes a specific next step you will take in sharing a verbal witness with seekers here:

Now go back through the previous exercise and select the one action item you intend to implement first. Write that sentence in the space provided on page 58 of this guide.

MAKE THE INVITATION

Bringing Seekers to Outreach Events, Seeker Small Groups, and Church Services

I always felt alone. No matter what relationship I was in, no matter what guy I was dating, no matter how many friends I had, I felt *alone*. Would I ever find a husband and have a family of my own? Would I ever find someone who would truly love me, someone to whom I could give my whole heart? In every relationship, I would push someone to love me, then give him reasons not to. Funny, huh? I sabotaged what I wanted. As much as I wanted to be loved, I felt I didn't deserve it. Again and again I found myself going through this endless, hopeless cycle.

But then something happened that eventually changed everything about who I was and what I thought I wanted in life. Over dinner one night, I told my friend Kim about my fears and loneliness. Get this—she used to deal with this exact same stuff! Then she said something a little odd. She told me that she was a Christian and that she prayed to God daily. And when she asked if she could include me in her prayers, I just about fell off my chair. I couldn't believe someone was actually going to spend time praying for me. I teased her about being religious, but inside I was touched. I found it hard to believe that someone who seemed to be as "together" as Kim would admit to something as ridiculous as religion, but something about it seemed genuine. I didn't tell her that, though.

I knew things were really getting bad when I accepted an offer from Kim to take in a church service. After spending the past year of our friendship pretty much just badgering, challenging, and belittling her faith, I was quite surprised that she even asked me. Even more surprising, I heard myself agree to go. Expecting to watch some kind of "touchy-feely, praise the Lord, oh, look how perfect we are" religious presentation, I was stunned by what I learned. The church wasn't some freak show for religious fanatics. In fact, the people there appeared completely normal. I sensed that some of them might have even had the same hang-ups, disappointments, and anxieties as me.

I was convinced during that service that something or someone was calling directly to me. The minister told us that a family from within the congregation suffered a tragedy the week before. Their five-year-old daughter had been killed in an auto accident. I remember wondering, "How could God allow a little child like that to die? Especially a child whose family had prayed so hard to adopt her. Didn't God know how much they loved her?" Then I found out that the parents of this little girl still kept their faith in God. Even though this tragedy happened in their life, they continued to love him—and they knew that he continued to love them. That was difficult to swallow, but I realized something: I wanted that. This love they relied on and expected and believed in—this was the kind of love I had been looking for my whole life.

After reflecting on my long list of stupid life choices, I decided to check out this church thing with Kim some more. I definitely needed some direction for my life, and this church seemed like a good place to get it. I ended up, months later, sitting in the service with Kim, crying, asking God to come into my life, and accepting Jesus as my Lord and Savior. I was twenty-nine years old and had never prayed before. It was amazing.

I've hardly missed a weekend service since. You may have seen me—I'm the one in the next-to-last row who's always crying by the end of the service. (I really need to remember to bring tissues, or at least to use waterproof mascara!) I am proof that God uses the church to touch people with the Gospel: I am one of those people, and I am so thankful.

I didn't used to think there was a God, but now I know there is because he has changed me! I'm learning to give up those relationship-destroying habits; God has begun to break that endless, hopeless cycle I've been in for so long. Sure I still struggle; I have a long way to go. But there's no denying the contentment I feel. It's amazing. When I finally understood what Jesus did for me, I chose to believe and open my heart to him. At that first service I attended, I remember the pastor talking about how that little girl would just walk right up to people and ask them if they believed in Jesus and how she would be seriously concerned for them if they didn't. Even in her death, that little girl still brought someone to Christ—me.

It scares me to think I might never have learned about how much Jesus loves me had my friend Kim not invited me to church. It was a risk she took—and I'm eternally grateful.

Open for Discussion

> How, then, can they call on the one they have not
> believed in? And how can they believe in the one of
> whom they have not heard? And how can they hear
> without someone preaching to them? And how can
> they preach unless they are sent? As it is written,
> "How beautiful are the feet of those
> who bring good news!"
>
> ROMANS 10:14–15 NIV

1. Think about the previous story and the process of bringing seekers to church services, small groups, or outreach events. What conclusions can you draw about the importance of inviting and bringing seekers to these things?

   What hinders you from inviting a seeking friend to a church service, a small group, or an outreach event?

2. Read Romans 10:14–15 on the previous page. Inviting seekers to outreach events, seeker small groups, or church services creates opportunities to have spiritual conversations with them. What additional benefits occur when we invite our seeker friends to church, small groups, or events designed especially for them?

3. Identify some fears or concerns a non-Christian might have about attending a seeker event, a seeker small group, or a church service with you.

4. A good way to invite seekers to a church service, a seeker small group, or an outreach event is to ensure them that they only need to come one time to check it out and see if this is something they would enjoy—with no obligation to return. This may ease the fears that seekers might have about accepting an invitation. What are some other things you could say to alleviate their fears?

5. Spending time with your seeking friends before and after the church service is one way to create a positive experience. What are some other things you could do to ensure a positive experience for the seekers you bring to services?

What guidelines (do's and don'ts) would you suggest concerning the time spent interacting with seekers?

Heart Check

6. An important element for seekers who come to church, small groups, or outreach events is follow-up. Getting together to discuss their thoughts and feelings about the experience goes a long way toward developing trust and openness with them. What kinds of follow-up questions could you ask your seeking friends that would encourage an ongoing dialogue around spiritual matters?

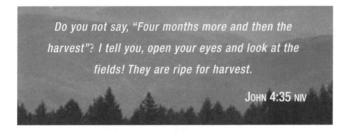

> *Do you not say, "Four months more and then the harvest"? I tell you, open your eyes and look at the fields! They are ripe for harvest.*
>
> JOHN 4:35 NIV

7. Read John 4:35 and Matthew 9:10–12. What attitude did Jesus display toward reaching seekers and the urgency of the Gospel message?

How can you safeguard against ever viewing seekers as "projects" as you make plans to invite them to a seeker event, a seeker small group, or a church service?

Personal Profile

The last time I saw Jay that year was at the end of the summer, just before we left for colleges in two different cities. After an exceptionally fierce tennis match, we shook hands, tossed our rackets into our cars, and had yet another one of those animated spiritual discussions. But this one was different. Jay seemed more intense than ever before, and his comments and questions seemed more focused—as if he was urgently looking for some answers. For the first time, he even appeared open to the idea that God might exist. Our conversation lasted until just past midnight, when we finally said goodbye and parted ways. Jay drove off in his car, and I climbed into mine and headed in the opposite direction.

As I came to a stop sign inside the park grounds, though, I suddenly couldn't drive any farther. An overwhelming sense of compassion for my friend welled up inside me, and I was unmistakably drawn to pray for him. I threw the car into park, and in front of that stop sign, bowed my head on the steering wheel, and said, "Oh God, please help Jay know that you're here. He seems so close and yet so far. His eyes are blinded to the truth about you. Open his eyes and help him to truly see you as you are."

It's hard to explain and impossible to prove, but in that moment of prayer, I sensed that God overwhelmingly cared for Jay. And that night I felt like I encountered the heart of God toward all seekers.

It was two years before I heard from Jay again. One day out of the blue, I heard his voice on the telephone:

"Hey, guess what!"

"Jay, is that you?"

"Yes. Guess what!"

"What?"

Jay related his story. "When I got here to college, I became friends with some students who happened to be Christians. Right away they invited me to join them for some small group discussions about the Bible and Christianity. So I decided to take them up on it and of course I brought all of my tough questions with me—you know, the same ones you never seemed to be able to answer!" (His competitive spirit was still intact.)

"After intensely wrestling with those spiritual issues," he continued, "I took a big step and decided there really might be a God out there after all. I started trying to figure out what he might be like and why he might act the way he does. I got to the point where I became convinced God not only existed, but that he actually cared about me. Eventually, I discovered it was possible to get to know God on a personal level, so I decided to ask Jesus Christ to be the forgiver and leader of my life. It took me two years to get to this point, but it was well worth the journey."

I was amazed—and thrilled! To think that I may have played a small role in seeing Jay come to Christ and have his whole life changed for all eternity was mind-boggling! A short time later, I stumbled upon a passage of Scripture that reminded me of my interactions with Jay. Psalm 126:5–6 (NIV) reads, "Those who sow in tears will reap with songs of joy. He who goes out weeping, carrying seed to sow, will return with songs of joy, carrying sheaves with him." This promise came true for me and has become for me a great source of encouragement with my ongoing efforts in evangelism.

And although I received that "Guess what!" phone call from Jay many years ago, to this day it still motivates me to keep reaching out to seekers. I'm reminded to hang out with seekers and drop those clues right away; to keep on praying and looking for open windows of opportunity to explain the Gospel; and to invite seeking friends to church services, seeker small groups, and outreach events.

And as if I needed additional motivation, I got a knock on my office door a while back from a pastor visiting Willow Creek during one of our conferences. He introduced himself and said, "I wanted to stop by and thank you for something. You see, your friend Jay led *me* to Christ. And it changed my life forever. I've been so impacted by the love of Christ that

I left the marketplace and now I want to do everything I can to help others find Christ too. So, thank you." That conversation settled it for me. Nothing compares to living a highly contagious Christian life.

8. Imagine that one of your seeking friends made a "Guess what!" phone call to you similar to the one in the story above. Describe what that experience might be like for you.

9. What is the role of prayer as it relates to the process of reaching out to seekers?

10. Describe the latest developments in the lives of the seekers with whom you are building friendships, sharing your faith, and bringing to outreach events, seeker small groups, and church services. As a group, spend time praying for those seekers whom you are hoping to reach for Christ.

Charting Your Journey

11. Check any of the statements below that describe the specific next steps you would like to work on and apply in your life at this point. Share your selection with the rest of the group and give reasons for your response.

❑ I will identify some guidelines for bringing seekers to church services, seeker small groups, or outreach events and share the guidelines with the rest of the group.

❑ My dream is to someday play a role in seeing someone come to Christ. I will pray about this daily.

❑ As I bring seekers to outreach events, seeker small groups, and church services, I will plan to meet with them afterward to follow up with them.

❑ Bringing seekers to the weekend services is a tool I can't afford to neglect. I will develop a plan for bringing as many seekers as possible to church services over the next six months.

❑ I will develop a list of fears that seekers might have about attending outreach events, seeker small groups, and church services—then I'll come up with ideas to alleviate those fears.

❑ As appropriate, I will ask those seekers with whom I have a high level of trust what is preventing them from crossing the line.

❑ I will ask my small group to hold me accountable for intentionally reaching out to the seekers around me.

❑ I will organize social gatherings before or after church services to which our small group can invite our seeking friends.

❑ Write your own phrase that describes a specific next step you will take in bringing seekers to outreach events or church services here:

Now go back through the previous exercise and select the one action item you intend to implement first. Write that sentence in the space provided on page 58 of this guide.

IMPACT LIST

These are the seekers I hope to see cross the line of faith someday. I will remember to pray for them on a regular basis.

1. _____

2. _____

3. _____

DO VS. DONE

NARRATIVE	OUTLINE
The difference between religion and Christianity is:	
Religion is spelled "D-O." It consists of trying to do enough good things to somehow please God, earn his forgiveness, and gain entrance into heaven. This self-effort plan can take on many forms, from trying to be a good, moral person to becoming an active participant in an organized religion—Christian or otherwise.	**RELIGION** • Is spelled "D-O" • Trying to do enough good things to please God
The problem is, we can never know when we have done enough. Even worse, the Bible makes it clear that we can *never* do enough in Romans 3:23: "For all have sinned and fall short of the glory of God." Simply put, the "D-O" plan cannot bring us peace with God, or even peace with ourselves.	**THE PROBLEM** • We can never know when we have done enough • The Bible says that we can *never* do enough (Romans 3:23)

Christianity, however, is spelled "D-O-N-E." In other words, that which we could never *do* for ourselves, Christ has already *done* for us. He lived the perfect life we could never live, and he died on the cross to pay for each of our wrongdoings. And now he freely offers us his gift of forgiveness and leadership for our lives.	**CHRISTIANITY**
	• Is spelled "D-O-N-E"
	• Christ did what we could never do
	  — Lived the perfect life we could not
	  — Died on the cross to pay for our wrongdoings

But it's not enough just to know this; we have to humbly receive what he has done for us. And we do that by asking for his forgiveness and leadership in our lives.	**OUR RESPONSE** • It's not enough just to know this • We have to receive what he has done for us by asking for his forgiveness and leadership in our lives
(At this point, ask a follow-up question like "Does this make sense to you?" or "What do you think about what I just said?")	**THEIR RESPONSE** • Does this make sense to you? • What do you think about what I just said?

THE THREE HABITS
OF HIGHLY CONTAGIOUS
CHRISTIANS

Here is an opportunity, before God and one another, to individually commit to specific action steps. In the spaces below, write the one specific next step you will take regarding each of the three habits of highly contagious Christians. Your prayerful decisions about how you will apply these sessions will go a long way toward developing an intentionally contagious Christian lifestyle.

Hang Out Together

1. With God's help and the support of my small group, I will, to the best of my ability, commit to building relationships with seekers. I will work toward accomplishing this goal by taking the following next step:

Look for Open Windows

2. With God's help and the support of my small group, I will, to the best of my ability, commit to sharing a verbal witness with seekers. I will work toward accomplishing this goal by taking the following next step:

Make the Invitation

3. With God's help and the support of my small group, I will, to the best of my ability, commit to bringing seekers to outreach events, seeker small groups, or church services. I will work toward accomplishing this goal by taking the following next step:

RECOMMENDED RESOURCES

Bill Hybels and Mark Mittelberg, *Becoming a Contagious Christian* (Grand Rapids: Zondervan, 1995).

Paul Little, *How to Give Away Your Faith* (Downers Grove, Ill.: InterVarsity, 1989).

Garry Poole, *Seeker Small Groups* (Grand Rapids: Zondervan, 2003).

Lee Strobel, *Inside the Mind of Unchurched Harry and Mary* (Grand Rapids: Zondervan, 1993).

Building Bridges of Trust That Lead People to Christ

SEEKER SMALL GROUPS
Garry Poole

Knocking on strange doors, handing out tracts, initiating engineered conversations—is that really what evangelism is all about? If you and those in your church get uncomfortable at the mere mention of the "E" word, then *Seeker Small Groups* will shift your whole concept to something different than anything you've ever experienced.

Right now there's someone in your circle of influence who could respond positively to the gospel—if only they found a nonthreatening way to explore spiritual issues honestly with others. *Seeker Small Groups* shows you how to reach unbelievers through small groups that meet their needs and help them encounter Christ.

A seeker small group is facilitated by a Christian leader, but the group members are seekers. The format gives non-Christians a safe place to come with their questions, objections, and obstacles and discuss spiritual matters on a regular basis. *Seeker Small Groups* will show you just how powerful and effective the seeker small group concept really is.

From the nuts and bolts of launching a seeker's group to the vision and values that will nurture an ongoing dialogue, *Seeker Small Groups* offers a proven way to reach out to those who are searching for spiritual answers and point them to Christ.

"In this excellent new book, Garry Poole passes on the practical wisdom he has gained from over twenty-five years of experience leading small groups in an evangelistic setting. I learned a great deal from *Seeker Small Groups* and recommend it."

—Nicky Gumbel, Founder and Director, The Alpha Course

Softcover
ISBN 0-310-24233-9

Pick up a copy at your favorite bookstore!

GRAND RAPIDS, MICHIGAN 49530 USA

WWW.ZONDERVAN.COM

*1001 Seeker-Friendly Questions to Initiate Fun
and Meaningful Conversations*

THE COMPLETE BOOK OF QUESTIONS

Garry Poole

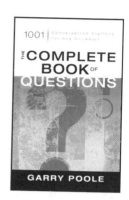

Everyone has a story to tell or an opinion to share. *The Complete Book of Questions* helps you get the conversational ball rolling. Created especially for seeker small groups, these questions can jump-start any conversation. They invite people to open up about themselves and divulge their thoughts, and provide the spark for stimulating discussions. This generous compilation of questions can be used in just about any context to launch great conversations.

Questions cover ten thematic categories, from light and easy questions such as, "What room in your house best reflects your personality?" to deeper, more spiritual questions such as, "If God decided to visit the planet right now, what do you think he would do?" *The Complete Book of Questions* is a resource that can help small group leaders draw participants out and couples, friends, and families get to know one another better.

Softcover
ISBN 0-310-24420-X

Pick up a copy at your favorite bookstore!

ZONDERVAN™

GRAND RAPIDS, MICHIGAN 49530 USA

WWW.ZONDERVAN.COM

TOUGH QUESTIONS

Garry Poole and Judson Poling

"The profound insights and candor captured in these guides will sharpen your mind, soften your heart, and inspire you and the members of your group to find vital answers together."

Bill Hybels

This second edition of Tough Questions, designed for use in any small group setting, is ideal for use in seeker small groups. Based on more than five years of field-tested feedback, extensive revisions make this best-selling series easier to use and more appealing than ever for both participants and group leaders.

Softcover

How Does Anyone Know God Exists?
ISBN 0-310-24502-8

What Difference Does Jesus Make?
ISBN 0-310-24503-6

How Reliable Is the Bible?
ISBN 0-310-24504-4

How Could God Allow Suffering and Evil?
ISBN 0-310-24505-2

Don't All Religions Lead to God?
ISBN 0-310-24506-0

Do Science and the Bible Conflict?
ISBN 0-310-24507-9

Why Become a Christian?
ISBN 0-310-24508-7

Leader's Guide
ISBN 0-310-24509-5

Pick up a copy at your favorite bookstore!

ZONDERVAN™

GRAND RAPIDS, MICHIGAN 49530 USA

WWW.ZONDERVAN.COM

WILLOW
Willow Creek Association

Willow Creek Association
Vision, Training, Resources for Prevailing Churches

This resource was created to serve you and to help you build a local church that prevails. It is just one of many ministry tools that are part of the Willow Creek Resources® line, published by the Willow Creek Association together with Zondervan.

The Willow Creek Association (WCA) was created in 1992 to serve a rapidly growing number of churches from across the denominational spectrum that are committed to helping unchurched people become fully devoted followers of Christ. Membership in the WCA now numbers over 10,500 Member Churches worldwide from more than ninety denominations.

The Willow Creek Association links like-minded Christian leaders with each other and with strategic vision, training, and resources in order to help them build prevailing churches designed to reach their redemptive potential. Here are some of the ways the WCA does that.

- **A2: Building Prevailing Acts 2 Churches—Today**—an annual two-and-a-half day event, held at Willow Creek Community Church in South Barrington, Illinois, to explore strategies for building churches that reach out to seekers and build believers, and to discover new innovations and breakthroughs from Acts 2 churches around the country.

- **The Leadership Summit**—a once a year, two-and-a-half-day conference to envision and equip Christians with leadership gifts and responsibilities. Presented live at Willow Creek as well as via satellite broadcast to over one hundred locations across North America, this event is designed to increase the leadership effectiveness of pastors, ministry staff, volunteer church leaders, and Christians in the marketplace.

- **Ministry-Specific Conferences**—throughout each year the WCA hosts a variety of conferences and training events—both at Willow Creek's main campus and offsite, across the U.S., and around the world—targeting church leaders and volunteers in ministry-specific areas such as: evangelism, small groups, preaching and teaching, the arts, children, students, women, volunteers, stewardship, raising up resources, etc.

- **Willow Creek Resources®**—provides churches with trusted and field-tested ministry resources in such areas as leadership, evangelism, spiritual formation, spiritual gifts, small groups, stewardship, student ministry, children's ministry, the use of the arts-drama, media, contemporary music —and more.

- **WCA Member Benefits**—includes substantial discounts to WCA training events, a 20 percent discount on all Willow Creek Resources®, *Defining Moments* monthly audio journal for leaders, quarterly *Willow* magazine, access to a Members-Only section on WillowNet, monthly communications, and more. Member Churches also receive special discounts and premier services through WCA's growing number of ministry partners—Select Service Providers—and save an average of $500 annually depending on the level of engagement.

For specific information about WCA conferences, resources, membership, and other ministry services contact:

Willow Creek Association
P.O. Box 3188
Barrington, IL 60011-3188
Phone: 847-570-9812
Fax: 847-765-5046
www.willowcreek.com